AN ABBEY THEATRE COMMISSION

DEATH OF A COMEDIAN

OWEN MCCAFFERTY

A co-production between the
Abbey Theatre, Soho Theatre and the Lyric Theatre

ABBEY
THEATRE
AMHARCLANN
NA MAINISTREACH

THE ABBEY THEATRE is Ireland's national theatre. It was founded by W.B. Yeats and Lady Augusta Gregory. Since it first opened its doors in 1904 the theatre has played a vital and often controversial role in the literary, social and cultural life of Ireland.

We place the writer and theatre-maker at the heart of all that we do, commissioning and producing exciting new work and creating discourse and debate on the political, cultural and social issues of the day. Our aim is to present great theatre in a national context so that the stories told on stage have a resonance with artists and audiences alike.

Death of a Comedian is Owen McCafferty's second play at the Abbey Theatre. His first play, *Quietly*, premiered on the Peacock stage in November 2012 and then toured to the Edinburgh Festival Fringe in 2013, where it won a Scotsman Fringe First Award. Owen won the 2013 Writers' Guild Award for Best Play for *Quietly*. In 2014, *Quietly* was performed at both the Lyric Theatre and Soho Theatre as part of a major Irish and international tour by the Abbey Theatre.

In 1905 the Abbey Theatre first toured internationally and continues to be an ambassador for Irish arts and culture worldwide. Over the years, the Abbey Theatre premiered the work of major playwrights such as J.M. Synge and Sean O'Casey and we continue to nurture relationships with important Irish writers.

None of this can happen without our audiences and our supporters. Annie Horniman provided crucial financial support to the Abbey in its first years. Many others have followed her lead by investing in and supporting our work.

We also acknowledge the financial support of the Arts Council.

An Roinn
Ealaíon, Oidhreachta agus Gaeltachta
Department of
Arts, Heritage and the Gaeltacht

The Abbey Theatre is funded by the Arts Council / An Chomhairle Ealaíon and receives financial assistance from the Department of Arts, Heritage and the Gaeltacht.

Archive partner of the Abbey Theatre

MEDIA SPONSORS
RTÉ
The Sunday Business Post

DIRECTOR'S CIRCLE
Bill Baroni
Richard Cawley
Dónall Curtin
Roma Downey
Basil Geoghegan
James Healy
Sen. Fiach Mac Conghail
James McNally
William O'Connor
Sheelagh O'Neill
Tom and Shelly O'Neill
Mark Ryan
Stabilis Capital Management
Gary and Anne Usling
Zachary Webb
Lloyd Weinreb

CORPORATE GUARDIANS
Accenture
Arthur Cox
Allianz
Bank of Ireland
Behaviour & Attitudes
Brown Thomas
Diageo Ireland
Electric Ireland
ESB
Irish Life
KPMG

McCann FitzGerald
Northern Trust
SIPTU
The Doyle Collection
Ulster Bank
Independent News & Media PLC

CORPORATE AMBASSADORS
Paddy Power
101 Talbot Restaurant
Bewley's
Wynn's Hotel
FCm Travel Solutions
Baker Tilly Ryan Glennon
CRH
Conway Communications
The Merrion Hotel
National Radio Cabs
The Church Bar & Restaurant
Clarion Consulting Limited
Manor House Hotels of Ireland
Spector Information Security
ely bar & brasserie
Zero-G
Irish Poster Advertising
DCC plc
Trocadero

FELLOWS
Frances Britton
Sherril Burrows
Catherine Byrne
The Cielinski Family
Tommy Gibbons
Pamela Fay
James Hickey
Dr. John Keane
Andrew Mackey
Eugene Magee
John & Irene McGrane
Gerard & Liv McNaughton
Donal Moore
Pat Moylan
Elizabeth Purcell Cribbin
Marie Rogan & Paul Moore

CORPORATE PARTNERS
High Performance
Executive Training

PROJECT SUPPORT
The Ireland Fund of Great Britain

London's most vibrant venue for new theatre, comedy and cabaret.

Soho Theatre is a major creator of new theatre, comedy and cabaret. Across our three different spaces we curate the finest live performance we can discover, develop and nurture. Soho Theatre works with theatre makers and companies in a variety of ways, from full producing of new plays, to co-producing new work, working with associate artists and presenting the best new emerging theatre companies that we can find. We have numerous writers and theatre makers on attachment and under commission, six young writers and comedy groups and we read and see hundreds of shows a year – all in an effort to bring our audience work that amazes, moves and inspires.

'Soho Theatre was buzzing, and there were queues all over the building as audiences waited to go into one or other of the venue's spaces. (The audience) is so young, exuberant and clearly anticipating a good time.' *Guardian*

We attract over 170,000 audience members a year.

We produced, co-produced or staged over forty new plays in the last twelve months.

Our social enterprise business model means that we maximise value from Arts Council and philanthropic funding; we actually contribute more to government in tax and NI than we receive in public funding.

sohotheatre.com

Keep up to date:
sohotheatre.com/mailing-list
facebook.com/sohotheatre
twitter.com/sohotheatre
youtube.com/sohotheatre

LOTTERY FUNDED | Supported using public funding by ARTS COUNCIL ENGLAND

PRINCIPAL SUPPORTERS

Nicholas Allott
Hani Farsi
Jack and Linda Keenan
Amelia and Neil Mendoza
Lady Susie Sainsbury
Carolyn Ward
Jennifer and Roger
Wingate

THE SOHO CIRCLE

Celia Atkin
Giles Fernando
Michael and Jackie Gee
Hedley and Fiona Goldberg
Tim Macready
Suzanne Pirret

CORPORATE SUPPORTERS

Adnams PLC
Bargate Murray
Bates Wells & Braithwaite
Cameron Mackintosh Ltd
EPIC Private Equity
Financial Express
Fisher Productions Ltd
Fosters
The Groucho Club
John Lewis Oxford Street
Latham & Watkins LLP
Lionsgate UK
The Nadler Hotel
Nexo
Oberon Books Ltd
Overbury Leisure
Publicis
Quo Vadis
Soho Estates
Soundcraft
SSE Audio Group

TRUSTS & FOUNDATIONS

The Andor Charitable Trust
The Austin and Hope
Pilkington Charitable Trust
Backstage Trust
Bertha Foundation
Boris Karloff Charitable
Foundation
Bruce Wake
Charitable Trust
The Buzzacott Stuart
Defries Memorial Fund
The Charles Rifkind
and Jonathan Levy
Charitable Settlement
The Coutts Charitable Trust
The David and Elaine
Potter Foundation
The D'Oyly Carte
Charitable Trust
The Ernest Cook Trust
The Edward Harvist Trust
The 8th Earl of Sandwich
Memorial Trust
Equity Charitable Trust
The Eranda Foundation
Esmée Fairbairn
Foundation
The Fenton Arts Trust
The Foundation for
Sport and the Arts
The Foyle Foundation
The Goldsmiths' Company
Harold Hyam Wingate
Foundation
Help A London Child
Hyde Park Place
Estate Charity
The Ian Mactaggart Trust
John Ellerman Foundation
John Lewis Oxford
Street Community
Matters Scheme
John Lyon's Charity

The John Thaw Foundation
JP Getty Jnr
Charitable Trust
The Kobler Trust
The Mackintosh
Foundation
The Mohamed S.
Farsi Foundation
The Rose Foundation
The Royal Victoria
Hall Foundation
St Giles-in-the-Fields
and William Shelton
Educational Charity
The St James's
Piccadilly Charity
Teale Charitable Trust
The Theatres Trust
The Thistle Trust
Unity Theatre
Charitable Trust
Westminster City Council-
West End Ward Budget
The Wolfson Foundation

SOHO THEATRE
BEST FRIENDS

Nick Bowers
Richard Collins
Miranda Curtis
Norma Heyman
Beatrice Hollond
David King
Lady Caroline Mactaggart
Hannah Pierce
Amy Ricker
Ian Ritchie and Jocelyne
van den Bossche
Ann Stanton
Alex Vogel
Sian and Matthew
Westerman
Hilary and Stuart Williams

In addition, we are immensely grateful to all of our DEAR FRIENDS and
GOOD FRIENDS, who support the work of Soho Theatre,
as well as those supporters who wish to remain anonymous.
For a full list of supporters please visit: www.sohotheatre.com/support-us/our-supporters

Lyric Theatre

The Lyric Theatre in Belfast makes a unique and vital contribution to the community as the only full-time producing theatre in Northern Ireland.

Employing local actors, including Liam Neeson, Ciarán Hinds and Adrian Dunbar at early stages of their careers, its mission is to produce high-quality professional theatre that is alive to the complex cultural experience and diverse traditions of Northern Ireland, and to use the power of live theatre to inspire, engage, educate and empower.

From first rehearsal to final curtain, the shows we create are truly indigenous products of Northern Ireland. Putting local issues and local characters centre stage is what the Lyric does best. Our shows are relevant to local audiences and revealing to visitors to the city. And a very important part of the Lyric Theatre's strategy is to tour as widely as possible, to give audiences outside Northern Ireland an insight into our culture and to the work of the Lyric.

Officially opened in May 2011 by Brian Friel, the Lyric's new home on the banks of Belfast's River Lagan, on the site of the previous theatre, is a landmark £18.1m building that signals the continued regeneration of the city and is a catalyst for real progress in arts infrastructure for artists and audiences alike.

Designed by O'Donnell + Tuomey, and built in a stunning blend of Belfast brick, glass, steel, concrete and Iroko timber, the new theatre is alive and dramatic at all times. Spacious lobbies and bars overlooking the river, and two beautiful auditoria with an exciting artistic programme, makes the Lyric a thriving social hub, creative learning space and a real attraction for visitors to the city.

PRINCIPAL FUNDER

MAIN STAGE SPONSOR

ALSO FUNDED BY

CORPORATE LOUNGE SPONSOR

AbbeyBondLovis

THE LYRIC IS ALSO GENEROUSLY SUPPORTED BY

CORPORATE STAR

IN-KIND SPONSOR

better fresher

DIRECTORS NOTE

WHEN I FIRST MOVED TO LONDON, one of the first shows I saw was Owen McCafferty's *Scenes from the Big Picture*. It was amazing. Superb acting. Some of the best I had seen. And a simplicity and truth of writing, that enabled actors to do what they do best. Not driven by clever narrative or tricksy staging - which was what I was into at the time - just a simple study of simple people faced with simple dilemmas.

Ten years later, as Artistic Director of Soho Theatre I sat mesmerized by the same writer, with the Abbey Theatre and Jimmy Fay's production of *Quietly*. Some of the same actors, exactly the same proposition, but ten years more craft, skill, insight and theatricality in the writing. Again, the actors flew.

When Fiach (Artistic Director of the Abbey Theatre) then agreed to collaborate with us to present *Quietly* at Soho (with the words "anywhere that's the English home of the Rubberbandits will do for me!"), I was delighted.

A short while later when Fiach sent a new play to myself and Jimmy (the newly appointed Executive Producer of the Lyric) by Owen called *Acting the Comedian*, they had us at "hello". Sometimes organisations are pushed to co-produce because of financial constraints and efficiency, this couldn't be further from our motivation on this new collaboration.

We have been rehearsing in London with Waterford, Walthamstow, Belfast, Sussex, Omagh, Derry, Wicklow and Shrewsbury in the room. It's a joke of its own waiting to be written.

The play itself is not about stand-up comedy. In the same way *Anthony and Cleopatra* isn't about Romans. It is, as ever with plays, about something much bigger. We have approached this story as a *Faust* or a *Macbeth* - anyone who takes on a noble ambition or has a good idea, and finds it gets corrupted or changed en route to its realisation. To use stand up as this metaphor places it as a noble ambition, with ideals - not always the attitude - but something that rings very true with Soho Theatre and the way we equally value all the artist across our stages, regardless of genre.

This is our second collaboration and hopefully a springboard to many, many more.

Steve Marmion
Artistic Director
Soho Theatre

cast (in order of appearance)

Comedian	Brian Doherty
Girlfriend	Katie McGuinness
Agent	Shaun Dingwall

production credits

Director	Steve Marmion
Set Design and Costume Design	Michael Vale
Lighting Design	Ben Ormerod
Sound Design	Tom Mills
Assistant Director	Sara Joyce
Voice Director	Andrea Ainsworth
Costume Supervisor	Sarah June Mills
Production Manager	Marty Moore
Casting Directors	Kelly Phelan
	Nadine Rennie
Company Stage Managers	Kate Miller
	Ashley Smith
Deputy Stage Manager	Tracey Lindsay
Assistant Stage Manager	Jean Hally
Relight technician	Kevin McFadden
Set Construction	Footprint Scenery
Set Graphic Design	Eliot Ruocco-Trenouth
Photography	Richard Davenport
	Ros Kavanagh

Biogra phies

OWEN MCCAFFERTY

WRITER

DEATH OF A COMEDIAN IS OWEN'S second play at the Abbey Theatre. His first play, *Quietly*, premiered on the Peacock stage in November 2012 and then toured to the Edinburgh Festival Fringe in 2013, where it won a Scotsman Fringe First Award. Owen won the 2013 Writers' Guild Award for Best Play for *Quietly*. In 2014, *Quietly* was performed at both the Lyric Theatre and Soho Theatre as part of a major Irish and international tour by the Abbey Theatre. Other previous work at the Lyric Theatre includes *The Absence of Women*. Other plays include *Titanic (Scenes from the British Wreck Commissioner's Inquiry, 1912)*, inaugural performance at MAC, Belfast, *Days of Wine and Roses* (Donmar Theatre), *Closing Time* (National Theatre London), *Shoot The Crow* (Druid and Prime Cut Productions, Belfast) and *Scenes From The Big Picture* (National Theatre London and Prime Cut Productions, Belfast), which won the Meyer-Whitworth, John Whiting and Evening Standard Awards. Owen is the only playwright to win these three major awards in one year for the same play. Over the last twenty years many of Owen's plays have been performed throughout Europe and have won various awards. Owen is currently the playwright-in-residence at the Lyric Theatre, Belfast.

BRIAN DOHERTY

COMEDIAN

BRIAN'S PREVIOUS APPEARANCES at the Abbey Theatre include *Three Sisters, Translations, Down the Line, Tarry Flynn, The Tempest* and *The Murphy Initiative*. He appeared at the Soho Theatre in *God in Ruins*(RSC). *Death of a Comedian* is his debut at the Lyric Theatre. Other theatre work includes *Antony and Cleopatra, The Winters Tale, Ahasverus, King Lear, Little Eagles, Julius Caesar, The Drunks, God in Ruins, Macbeth, Macbett* and *Great Expectations* (Royal Shakespeare Company), *Aristocrats* (National Theatre, London) *From Here To Eternity, Stones in His Pockets* (West End), *Famine* (Druid Theatre), *Improbable Frequency, Pentecost, Boomtown, The School for Scandal* (Rough Magic), *Zoe's Play* (The Ark), *Romantic Friction* (Read Company), *Macbeth* (Second Age), *Emma* (Storytellers), *Amphibians* (Tin Drum), *Studs* (The Passion Machine), *Car Show* (The Corn Exchange), *Conquest of the South Pole* (Theatre Demo), *Narrative* (Royal Court Theatre), *A Steady Rain* and *The Father* (Theatre Royal Bath). He was also a founder member of Red Kettle Theatre Company and appeared in many of their productions including *Talbot's Box, The Glass Menagerie, The Crucible, The Blackpool, Observe the Sons of Ulster Marching Towards the Somme* and *Happy Birthday Dear Alice*. Film and television credits include *Raw, Perriers Bounty, Pure Mule, Garage, Fair City, Casualty, Law and Order UK, Billy the Kid, Doctors, The Clinic, The Bombmaker, Glenroe* and *The Chief.*

SHAUN DINGWALL

AGENT

THIS IS SHAUN'S DEBUT at the Abbey Theatre, Lyric Theatre and Soho Theatre. Other plays include *Sixty-Six Books* (Bush Theatre), *The Man Who Had All The Luck* (Donmar Warehouse) and *Beautiful Thing* (Bush Theatre at Donmar Warehouse), *Incomplete Random Acts of Kindness* (Royal Court Theatre), *Henry IV part 1 and 2* (Bristol Old Vic) and *Troilus and Cressida* (The Old Vic). TV work includes *The Driver, The Long Firm, New Tricks, Rock and Chips, In a Land of Plenty, Crime and Punishment, Spooks, Survivors, Moses Jones, Charles II: The Power and the Passion, Doctor Who* and *Leaners* (BBC), *Poirot, The Suspicions of Mr Whicher,*

Breathless, Above Suspicion, Vera and *Midsomer Murders* (ITV). Film work includes *Tomorrow La Scala, On a Clear Day, Summer in February* and *The Forgotten,* which is yet to be released.

KATIE MCGUINNESS

GIRLFRIEND

THIS IS KATIE'S DEBUT at the Abbey Theatre, Lyric Theatre and Soho Theatre. Other plays include *The Drowned Man: A Hollywood Fable* (Punchdrunk/National Theatre) *An Inspector Calls* (National Theatre UK Tour), *The Stepmother, Mary Broome, Chains of Dew* and *Tragedy of Nan* (Orange Tree Theatre), *Life for Beginners* and *Decade* (Theatre 503), *Yesterday* (Young Vic/Theatre Uncut), *Sixty-Six Books* (Bush), *Prophesy* (Public Theater NYC), *Reclining Nude with Black Stockings* (Arcola), *The Sock* (Nabokov), *As You Like It* (Sprite Productions), *Balmoral* (Theatre Royal, Bath), *A History of Falling Things* (Theatre Clwyd), *Living Quarters* (Royal Lyceum), *Salome* (Nuffield) *Much Ado About Nothing* (Salisbury Playhouse) and *Romeo and Juliet* (Vienna's English Theatre). Television and Film work includes *The Borgias, Lewis, Dirty Filty Love, MIT, He Knew*

He Was Right, Every Seven Seconds, Hotel Babylon, Bombil and Beatrice, The Spy, A Performance and *The Night Hag.*

STEVE MARMION

DIRECTOR

STEVE IS ARTISTIC DIRECTOR of Soho Theatre. For Soho Theatre, Steve has directed *The One, Pastoral,* the French and English productions of *Address Unknown, Realism* (Whatsonstage Award-nominated), *Mongrel Island, Fit and Proper People* (with the RSC), *Utopia, The Boy Who Fell Into A Book* and *Late Night Gimp Fight.* Prior to joining the company in 2010, Steve directed *Macbeth* for Regent's Park Open Air Theatre and *Dick Whittington, Jack and the Beanstalk* and *Aladdin* for the Lyric Hammersmith. In 2009 he directed the highly successful production of *Edward Gant's Amazing Feats of Loneliness* for Headlong Theatre which received rave reviews on tour and at Soho Theatre. In 2008 he had three critically praised successes with *Vincent River* in New York, *Only the Brave* in Edinburgh and *Metropolis* in Bath. He also transferred Rupert Goold's *Macbeth* onto Broadway. Steve was assistant, then Associate Director, at the RSC over two years from 2006-07. In 2004 he directed several premieres for Sir Alan Ayckbourn at the Stephen Joseph Theatre and returned to direct the Christmas show in 2006. *Only the Brave* (2008) was nominated for Best New Musical and Best New Music and his *Madam Butterfly's Child* (2004) and *Mad Margaret's Revenge* (2005) won the London One Act Theatre Festival. Prior to this he was Youth Theatre Director at Theatre Royal Plymouth and The Sherman. He has worked with the National Theatre, RSC, in the West End, on Broadway, at the Royal Court, Lyric Hammersmith, Theatre Royal Plymouth, Theatre Royal Bath, Watford Palace Theatre, Sherman Theatre Cardiff and Edinburgh Festival.

MICHAEL VALE
SET AND COSTUME DESIGN

MICHAEL HAS DESIGNED the sets and costumes for over 200 theatre and opera productions both in the UK and abroad including those he has directed. Companies he has worked with include: The Royal Shakespeare Company; The National Theatre; The Royal Opera House; English National Opera; Glyndebourne Festival Opera; Opera North; English Touring Opera; De Vlaamse Opera, Antwerp; Los Angeles Opera; New Zealand International Art's Festival; Galaxy Theatre, Tokyo; Warsaw Globe Theatre Company; Munich Biennalle; Lyric Hammersmith; The Royal Court; Almeida Theatre; Soho Theatre; Manchester Royal Exchange; Birmingham Rep.; West Yorkshire Playhouse; Sheffield Crucible; Northampton Theatre Royal; Liverpool Playhouse; Nottingham Playhouse; Bristol Old Vic; Plymouth Theatre Royal; Edinburgh Royal Lyceum; Bolton Octagon; Oldham Coliseum; Manchester Library Theatre; Salisbury Playhouse; Colchester Mercury Theatre; English Touring Theatre; The Royal Festival Hall; The Queen Elizabeth Hall; The Sage, Gateshead; Battersea Arts Centre; Spymonkey; Kneehigh Theatre Company and Told By An Idiot, with whom he is an Associate Idiot. His work has been nominated for two Olivier Awards; an Irish Times Theatre Award; a Manchester Evening News Theatre Award, a Charrington Fringe First Award and two Off West End Theatre Awards.

BEN ORMEROD
LIGHTING DESIGNER

BEN'S PREVIOUS WORK at the Abbey Theatre includes *She Stoops to Conquer, Translations, The Big House, The Importance of Being Earnest, The Freedom of the City* (also New York), *The Colleen Bawn, The House, The Wake* and *Made in China* at the Soho Theatre he has designed *The One* and at the Lyric Theatre he designed *The Crucible*. Other theatre work includes *The Herbal Bed* (Clwyd), *Zorro* (West End/Paris/Japan/US), *Serious Money, Last Easter* (Birmingham Rep), *Dimetos* (Donmar), *Two Men of Florence* (Boston), *The Dresser* (Watford), *Legal Fictions* (West End), *Macbeth* (Albery), *The Leenane Trilogy* (Druid Theatre Company/Royal Court/Broadway), *A Midsummer Night's Dream, The Merchant of Venice, The Winter's Tale, Twelfth Night* and *Rose Rage* (Propeller Theatre Company, also New York/Chicago), *The Heresy of Love, Macbeth, The Revenger's Tragedy, Henry V, Julius Caesar, The Spanish Golden Age Season* (RSC), *Bent, Uncle Vanya, The Winter's Tale, In Remembrance of Things Past* (National Theatre, London), *The Changeling, Hedda Gabler, A Doll's House* and *The Seagull* (English Touring Theatre). Opera credits include *The Ring of the Nibelung* (Longborough), *La Traviata* (Denmark), *Jeanne d'Arc au Bucher* (Rome), *Falstaff, Cosi fan tutti, Il trovatore* (Scottish Opera), *La Traviata* (ENO), *The Turn of the Screw* (Bath/Wessex), *Baa Baa Black Sheep* (Opera North/BBC2), *Punch and Judy* (Aldeburgh) and *The Mask of Orpheus* (BBC Symphony Orchestra). Dance includes *Casse Noisette* and *Les Noces* (Geneva), *Frame of View* (Cedar Lake Contemporary Ballet, New York), *See Blue Through* (Ballet Gulbenkian, Introdans/Phoenix), *Tender Hooks* (Skånes Dans Teater/Ballet Gulbenkian) and *Cinderella* (Göteborg). Ben has also designed the lighting for the *Calico Museum of Textiles, Ahmedabad*, directed Athol Fugard's *Dimetos* at the Gate Theatre, London and adapted four films from Kieslowski's *Dekalog for E15*.

TOM MILLS
SOUND DESIGNER

TOM'S PREVIOUS WORK at Soho Theatre includes *The Night Before Christmas, Pastoral, The Boy Who Fell Into A Book, Utopia, Boys, Realism, Mongrel Island* and *Amazing Feats of Loneliness. Death* of a Comedian is his debut at the Abbey Theatre and the Lyric Theatre. Other theatre credits include *Arabian Nights adventure in learning* (Birmingham Rep/Library), *Dirty Butterfly, Far Away, A Streetcar Named Desire* (Young Vic), *The Importance of Being Earnest* (West End/Tour), *Birdland, A Time To Reap* (Royal Court), *First Encounters of the Taming of The Shrew, Titus Andronicus* (RSC), *Enjoy* (WYP), *King Lear* (Bath), *Bottleneck* (Hightide), *Rock Pool* (UK Tour), *Cinderella* (Lyric Hammersmith), *The Alchemist* (Liverpool Playhouse), *Medea* (Headlong), *The Dark at The Top of The Stairs* (Belgrade, Coventry).

year she directed *Click* by Kate Kennedy and *The Playboy Variations*, new short plays by emerging Irish Writers. Other directing credits include *Cloud 9, The Wonderful World of Dissocia, Attempts On Her Life* and *Lunch*.

SARA JOYCE

ASSISTANT DIRECTOR

SARA STUDIED DRAMA and Theatre at Trinity College, Dublin and then trained at École Jacques Lecoq. She is co-founder of Whispering Beasts Theatre Company, winners of Deutsche Bank Award for Drama 2013. She has worked with Steve Marmion and Soho Theatre on several productions, including directing the Soho Young Playwrights showcase, which she will direct again in June. Sara is especially excited by new writing. Last

Death of a Comedian

Over the last twenty years Owen McCafferty's plays
have been performed throughout Europe and have won
various awards. Previous work includes *Titanic* (*Scenes
from the British Wreck Commissioner's Inquiry, 1912*),
the inaugural performance at MAC, Belfast; *The Absence
of Women* (Lyric Theatre, Belfast, and Tricycle Theatre,
London); *Days of Wine and Roses* (Donmar Theatre);
Closing Time (National Theatre, London); *Shoot the
Crow* (Druid and Prime Cut Productions, Belfast); *Mojo
Mickybo* (Kabosh); *Scenes from the Big Picture* (National
Theatre, London, and Prime Cut Productions, Belfast),
which won the Meyer-Whitworth, John Whiting and
Evening Standard Awards; and *Quietly* (Abbey Theatre,
Dublin), which won the Writers' Guild Award for Best
Play. *Death of a Comedian* is a co-production between
Abbey Theatre, Lyric Theatre and Soho Theatre. Owen
is an Associate Artist with Prime Cut Productions and
Playwright in Residence at the Lyric Theatre.

OWEN McCAFFERTY

Death of a Comedian

FABER & FABER

First published in 2015
by Faber and Faber Limited
74–77 Great Russell Street
London WC1B 3DA

Typeset by Country Setting, Kingsdown, Kent CT14 8ES
Printed in England by CPI Group (UK) Ltd, Croydon, Surrey CRO 44Y

A CIP record for this book
is available from the British Library

ISBN 978–0–571–32553–5

FSC
www.fsc.org
MIX
Paper from
responsible sources
FSC® C101712

2 4 6 8 10 9 7 5 3 1

Author's Notes

The play never breaks stride. The Comedian moves from conversations to gigs seamlessly.

The conversations the Comedian has with his Girlfriend and the Agent happen around him. There is no need for them to be seen as 'proper' scenes.

The Comedian is always either 'offstage' (in conversation or warming up for a gig) or 'onstage' (doing a 'live' gig and talking directly to the audience).

The Comedian rarely moves from centre stage. It's as if the spotlight is on him all the time (though it isn't).

The venues the Comedian is playing get progressively bigger – he starts off in a small dingy comedy club and ends up somewhere like the Apollo in London.

At the start and end of each gig there will be appropriate canned laughter.

Death of a Comedian, a co-production between the Abbey Theatre, Dublin, Soho Theatre, London, and the Lyric Theatre, Belfast, was first performed on the Danske Bank stage of the Lyric Theatre, Belfast, on 7 February 2015. The cast was as follows:

Comedian Brian Doherty
Girlfriend Katie McGuinness
Agent Shaun Dingwall

Director Steve Marmion
Set and Costume Design Michael Vale
Lighting Design Ben Ormerod
Sound Design Tom Mills
Assistant Director Sara Joyce
Voice Director Andrea Ainsworth
Costume Supervisor Sarah June Mills
Production Manager Marty Moore
Casting Directors Kelly Phelan, Nadine Rennie

Characters

The Comedian
The Girlfriend
The Agent

DEATH OF A COMEDIAN

The Comedian is practising the noise he will make later in the play.

Comedian   fuck

He practises again.

fuck i hate this

what if i'm not funny

Girlfriend   you are funny

Comedian   what does that mean

Girlfriend   you're a funny person

Comedian   a funny person – i don't want to be a funny person i want to be a comedian

Girlfriend   go out there and be funny then

Comedian   what if i'm not funny though – what if i go out there and i'm not funny

Girlfriend   you will be

Comedian   how do you know

Girlfriend   you've done it before – i watched it – you were funny

Comedian   yes i have been funny – there's a few times though i wasn't funny enough – it was me – it wasn't the audience it was me – i knew it – picked the wrong moments to try new material out – didn't structure the set

properly – should've eased the new material
in – bit by bit – in between gags i knew
worked – my fault – stupid – i hate that –
i hate when i do that – one of the things i
have to teach myself is to be in control all
the time – never panic – never chase laughs –
it wasn't that the new material wasn't funny –
i didn't work it properly – good material
wasted – i hate that – wasted – useless –
part of it was about how politicians when
they're asked a question they can't answer
all make the same noise – it's like a big
bucket of water on the boil

He makes the noise.

there was more to it than that – it was
about them all being duplicitous bastards –
but that noise – that was the thing that was
recognisable in it – that's funny isn't it – that
noise i mean – it's funny

Girlfriend	in front of an audience it feels like it'll be funny – it's not funny now
Comedian	no

He makes the same noise.

i heard on the way in there might be an
agent in here tonight

Girlfriend	there's always an agent might be in
Comedian	yes – which means there might be one in tonight
Girlfriend	to watch you
Comedian	maybe
Girlfriend	good

Comedian	good – good – what if i'm not funny
Girlfriend	if you're not funny you're fucked
Comedian	very good
Girlfriend	i know – but at the moment we're somewhere in between me wanting with every sinew of my body to help you and – hitting you the biggest slap round the head i can muster up
Comedian	that's good though – i need that edge
Girlfriend	i'm not joking about the slap by the way
Comedian	i know – the agent might be here to see me
Girlfriend	is that what you heard
Comedian	no
Girlfriend	right
Comedian	i feel like it might be the right time – i feel like i'm starting to get on top of my material – not just about it being funny – it has to be that – that's a given – i'm a comedian for fuck sake – i mean about what i'm getting at – how i see the world is starting to come through
Girlfriend	yes it is
Comedian	it is isn't it
Girlfriend	yes
Comedian	really
Girlfriend	yes – i admire that in you – it can't be easy to stand in front of a group of strangers and tell them what you think about

Comedian	you've never said that to me before
Girlfriend	i think it's starting to kick in what it is you do – plus i also think about stuff in roughly the same way you do – although in a better way
Comedian	i might start using us as material
Girlfriend	don't even joke about that
Comedian	i wouldn't – we're not cutting edge enough
Girlfriend	don't worry about the agent
Comedian	i'm not – i am but i'm not – i'm funny – i know that – whether there's an agent in the audience tonight or not i still need one in order to move on – can't play dives all the time – the wrong people sometimes – it can't stay like this
Girlfriend	no – although it does for some comedians – there's nothing wrong with knowing and staying at your own level
Comedian	i'm not like that
Girlfriend	no – but there's something i need to be clear about
Comedian	i won't forget you when i'm famous
Girlfriend	i need to know . . .
Comedian	that was a joke
Girlfriend	i need to know that you're doing this for the right reasons
Comedian	why
Girlfriend	because i'm doing it with you

Comedian	i'm trying to make a career
Girlfriend	that's not what i mean
Comedian	does this have to be now
Girlfriend	an agent might be in – this might be the start – yes now – just before you go on – i need to know why this is important – i'm going to play second fiddle – i don't mind that but i have to know why you're doing this
Comedian	to be funny and to be heard
Girlfriend	right
Comedian	and make a few quid
Girlfriend	the sooner you do that the better
Comedian	no pressure – right better start getting ready – you going to watch
Girlfriend	you want me to
Comedian	yes – stand at the back – have a drink – look out for the agent
Girlfriend	how will i know
Comedian	they'll look like an agent
Girlfriend	what's that
Comedian	the devil with a smile – maybe a bit of bling – entertainment
Girlfriend	you're funny
Comedian	i know – tell me you love me
	She kisses him.
Girlfriend	i love you

*Comedian prepares himself – makes the
noise he previously made.*

Comedian   we live in a world – what type of fucking
world do we live in – shit i knew this an
hour ago – hypocrisy – greed – poverty –
oppression – brutality – right – fuck –
shouldn't have said that – why do i always
say that – (*Makes the noise.*) walk on say
what you have to say and walk off – what
was all that shit about doing this for the
right reasons – found out i could do
something so i'm doing it – doesn't go any
further than that at the moment – all
politicians are cunts – that's it – got it – right

good evening

Silence – timing.

all politicians are cunts – even the good ones
– they're not people any more – can't talk –
you know the way you meet someone and
you say to them how's it going – they go –
fine i'm going down to the shops to buy
some cups – or whatever it is you kids are
calling drugs these days – you ask a politician
how it's going and it's all fucking texts to
the party whip – is it the party whip – that
suits those people down to the ground
doesn't it – the party – whip – the spin
doctor – party – whip – spinning – who
wouldn't want that job – and even within
that there's a safety net – too much partying
whipping or spinning and who's there on
hand but a – doctor – if you went to your
own doctor and told him you were sore
from whipping he'd tell you to fuck off –

those words – they're fucking taunting us –
he just asked me how's it going – spin
doctor – whatever the fuck you do don't
give a direct answer – the last time this
happened and someone gave a direct answer
it was all cup cakes leather chaps talc and
horse semen – fucking disaster – it's going
the way it has previously gone and no doubt
will go in the future – they all make the
same noise don't they – when they won't or
can't answer something they all make the
same noise – (*Makes the noise.*) it's like
bubbling fucking water or something –
(*Noise.*) why have we gone to war – (*Noise.*)
why is the gap between the rich and the
poor always increasing – (*Noise.*) why are
you afraid of those media fucks – (*Noise.*)
why do you encourage a society where the
rich and sometimes the not so rich blame
the fucking poor for all the world's ills –
(*Big noise.*) and we allow them to get away
with it in a way we wouldn't allow
ourselves to – imagine how ludicrous and
absurd it would be if any time things got a
bit hairy – that's what's wrong isn't it to
politicians everything is a bit hairy – when
things got a bit hairy in your own life and
you used the noise – you weren't in until
three o'clock this morning where were you –
(*Noise.*) i left half a bottle of milk in the
fridge to make pancakes this morning
because it's pancake tuesday – where's the
milk you dickhead – (*Noise.*) there was
more lube in that tube than there is now –
where'd it go – (*Noise.*) all arguments in
relationships are about where things go or

where they've been or where they are –
where where where – a long time married
couple are sitting at the breakfast table –
very middle class – actually sitting to eat –
one of them is trying to make an effort the
other isn't – knock knock – fuck off –
people in power are advertising themselves –
that's what this is all about – they want to
tell us how good and kind they are – doesn't
really matter if they can't do their job or
ignore the punters who voted for them as
long as we think they are good and kind –
consequently they have no fucking
personalities – like ads on the tv they're just
selling – no fucking character – that's why
they can't tell the truth – or feel the need to
protect us from the truth – it's fucked – the
war on drugs – a war – what the fuck is
that – i was sitting having a pint the other
day and this guy beside me – you know the
way if you have a pint in front of you and
someone buys you another one – doesn't
happen all over the world i know that –
mainly to do with here – what you do is
pour some of the new pint into the old one
to top it up – this guy was so drunk he
poured a full pint into a full pint – the
whole fucking thing – there should be a war
on that – can't – tax – imagine a politician
showing a delegate of chinese businessmen
the local area to see if they wanted to invest
and bringing them out for lunch in a nice
pub – a bit of culture – the chinese guy asks
why is that man – of working age – pouring
a full container of liquid into another full
container of liquid – (*Noise.*) no mention of

course of the chinese killing female babies –
just as long as we make money from them –
i don't have any money – as a person i don't
have any money – don't know why i said
that – as a person – of course as a person –
take it for granted that i don't mean me as a
house or a packet of condoms doesn't have
any money – i don't have any money – why
the fuck is that – why is it all the dickheads
have the money – you can all try this – this
is a bit of audience participation – there's
a thing called the dickhead list – there's
certain people when you say their name you
automatically follow with – dickhead – try
it – see – jeremy kyle – dickhead – george
osborne – dickhead – louis walsh – there's
some of them there's no need to even say it
you just know – none of them skint – what's
going on – ordinary people knocking their
pan in for pennies and we pay these fuckers
fortunes for at best mediocrity at worst
failure – put them all on minimum wage see
how things would change then – the gap
between the rich and the poor would close a
bit i think – a little less – (*Noise.*) then – any
war get the people in power to send their
kids – first in the firing line – not so fucking
gung ho then i think – and then the church
tells us it's alright to be poor – what chance
have you got – there's another group that
needs to be liked – breakfast presenters –
what the fuck is going on there – like a
school for bad actors or something – they
do this thing with their faces to let you know
that something's really sad – or something
really bad – or when they're glad – sad bad

and glad – they don't really want to tell you
anything other than they've just run the
marathon – and that that means they're a
good person when in fact they're just
numbing the fuck out of everything – can you
do that – numb the fuck out of something –
today bad shit happened somewhere – bad
face – something happened to some children –
sad face – and people we don't give a fuck
about either got married or split up – glad
face – and finally i've run the marathon –
thank you for noticing me – thank you
thank you thank you – fucking exhausting –
i'm going to finish with a joke – funny thing
for a comedian to say that isn't it – the
assumption being that i haven't been telling
jokes up to this point – for those of you
who think i haven't – just so i let you know
my line of work – i'm going to finish with a
joke – the only reason i'm finishing with it is
because i like it – not that i don't like the
stuff i've already done – if i keep going like
this i'm going get on to the dickhead list
aren't i – right – this man is looking to buy
a racehorse – this man – let's call him – a
complete cunt – so a complete cunt wants
to buy a racehorse – he doesn't want a
racehorse because he needs one – he has
too much money and he heard other people
with too much money have them so he
wanted one – he wasn't even sure what they
do – other than race – possibly against other
horses – he assumed they fed themselves but
what they eat he had no idea – so a complete
cunt who knows nothing about racing
horses wants to buy a racehorse – where

would such a person look – once he had
removed his head from up his arse because
there was no racehorses up there he looked
in the local newspaper under items for sale –
chance would have it that the day he looked
was the first day in the one hundred year
history of the local newspaper that there
was a horse for sale in the items for sale
section – he until the day he died because he
didn't read that newspaper again thought
that was how people sold racehorses – the
ad read – racehorse for sale fifty five walmer
street – he didn't know where walmer street
was so he took a taxi – it was in what elvis
would've called a ghetto – so now this
complete cunt thought that working class
people sold racehorses – he called at fifty
five walmer street and an old lady answered
the door – she was a decent old lady who
had looked after this horse all her adult life –
the house she lived in was a small terraced
house that had only a yard to separate it
from the house behind – do you have a
horse for sale – yes son i do – a racehorse –
yes a racehorse – they go out to the yard to
inspect the horse – the horse looks like it
might've been in a car accident – if indeed
it was the type of horse that drove a car –
the complete cunt thought she thinks i'm a
complete cunt while i may be a complete
cunt i still know what racehorses look like –
this isn't a racehorse the complete cunt said –
yes it is said the decent old woman – she
opens the yard door – this is where you
need imagination – right – outside the yard
was a massive green open field – at the

bottom of this open field stood a single huge oak tree – the decent old woman said this is the fastest horse you'll ever see – the complete cunt didn't believe her – because he was a complete cunt – the decent old woman slapped the horse on the arse and it bolted out of the yard and into the field at a hundred miles an hour – it is indeed the fastest horse god ever pumped breath into – across the field it gallops at the speed of light and runs head first straight into the oak tree – why does he do that said the complete cunt – i don't know said the decent old woman he just doesn't give a fuck – thank you and good night

fuck it – fuck it – you pour some of the old pint into the new pint to top it up – i said it back to front – fuck it – was the agent there

Girlfriend maybe

Comedian fuck – it wasn't good

Girlfriend it was good

Comedian i didn't hide myself enough – kept pushing its way through – i'm thinking – easy – easy – then bang – we're killing children in china

Girlfriend it's what you think

Comedian fuck what i think

Girlfriend one sniff of an agent and you're already starting to lose sight here

Comedian don't be ridiculous – what about the joke – too much complete cunt

Girlfriend people laughed – i don't know

Comedian	you're meant to be helping me
Girlfriend	right – help you – you're a fuck up – the problem is you're a good fuck up – i see that in you maybe others don't – when we first met i wanted to slap you a lot – you still make me want to slap you but not as often – over the few years we have been together i have slowly come to understand that for me that's love – so if they were doing a remake of the love story and you and i were in it the line would now be – love is not wanting to slap you as much as i used to
Comedian	you're a funny person
Girlfriend	yes – does that annoy you
Comedian	sometimes
Girlfriend	good – you torture me – you don't see this but that's difficult to take – you have to get used to it – you have to find a reason to get used to it – so you have to wait – wait and see what comes along – stand up comedy – when you said i want to do stand up i immediately thought of course you do – so here we are – you're still a fuck up – you still torture me – and now you're a stand up – one who mostly performs in shitholes late at night when the audience are laughed out and drunk – but a stand up nonetheless – so i come with you and watch – and besides all the good times – like driving in the middle of the night watching you sleep and listening to you snore because you downed half a bottle of gin – which i don't mind i like that world – i watch and i see something in you – something that needs to come out –

and i realise when i'm watching you that as
well as torturing me you torture yourself
and i like that about you – i love that about
you – i love you because you're prepared to
torture yourself – does that help

Comedian yes

Girlfriend and to answer your question – it was a good
set – you were funny – but it wasn't a good
enough set and you weren't funny enough
for you – and i could see that you only told
the joke because you had lost your way and
you needed to remind the audience that you
were funny and instead of pushing on you
bottled it and decided to tell a joke – you
see the world the way i see it – that's what
helps between the two of us – you're trying
to say something that matters to you – i like
that – if you're asking me what i think's
wrong i'll tell you – it all feels too raw – it's
not what you're saying but sometimes how
you say it – and how you link what it is you
want to say – this is the right time for me to
say this – you're not working hard enough –
i don't mean putting the hours in on stage –
i mean thinking – work out what you're
doing – sit down and work it out – make
yourself better – there's a trick to this – you
need to make yourself better without losing
sight of who you are – that's what i'm
waiting on you to do – that's why i'm still
here – funny man

The Agent enters.

Agent i hope i'm not interrupting – as a person i
don't like being interrupted myself so i am

26

always very aware that others' lives are
happening at the same time as mine – or to
put it another way – it's not always about me
– my name is doug wright – i'm an agent –
maybe you have heard of me

Comedian   yes of course i have

Agent   so you know why i'm here then (*To
            Girlfriend.*) sorry i'm so ignorant

            *He shakes her hand then kisses her on the
            cheek.*

            you smell beautiful – i like that in a person –
            sometimes i think the world can smell too
            real – you didn't say your name on stage –
            you should always say your name on stage –
            make it personal – steve

            They shake hands.

            steve – steve – steve

Comedian   steve johnston

Agent   yes steve johnston – steve johnston – i don't
            see it yet – but these things take time

Girlfriend maggie fairbrother

Agent   the beautiful smelling maggie – now let's get
            down to business – you're good but that
            doesn't really mean anything does it – good
            isn't a – thing – now the things are – good
            translates as not good enough . . .

Girlfriend what's happening here – have you decided
            something here that we're not aware of

Agent   oh right – i thought we all understood each
            other

Girlfriend	we don't know each other
Agent	we don't have to know each other to understand each other – my fault – i can be a bit ahead of the game sometimes – i thought because steve had heard of me – you did say you had heard of me steve didn't you
Comedian	yes of course i have – you're one of if not the main agent
Agent	one of – let's be humble – i thought you knew the way i operated – sorry i've made you uncomfortable – the last thing i want maggie is to make either of you uncomfortable – only the opposite is true – is there anything you want to ask – it's just i think there's a lot of time that can be wasted at moments like this – thinking thinking thinking thinking – it's all needless and messy – let's just do some business – i'm about business
Girlfriend	who else do you represent
Agent	good question maggie – the short answer is whoever i want – are you steve's manager maggie
Girlfriend	we don't see it like that – we do everything together – a team
Agent	team steve johnston – lovers
Girlfriend	we are in a relationship
Agent	good stuff – that often works – a good solid understanding reliable partner in the background – keeping the machine oiled – you haven't spoken steve – i've noticed that

Comedian	parts of tonight's set are annoying me
Agent	that's what's important steve – that's why i'm here – let's talk about tonight – sorry before i go on – to answer your early question maggie – all the main ones – i represent all the main ones – big venues – tv – that's my game – steve you have a way with you – don't take this the wrong way – what you say is important – what you say is part of you – but what's more important is how you say it – a good comic can make anything funny – that's what i see in you – i saw a grain of that tonight in your performance – the ability to make anything funny – priceless – all the greats have it – what you decide to make funny is your business – that's who you are – whatever it is inside you will come out – part of your job is to hide it
Comedian	i knew that – didn't i say that – tonight i didn't hide myself well enough – that comes with time though
Agent	yes of course it does – i've worked with comedians who were a lot worse than you at this point – right tonight – what did you think of tonight maggie
Girlfriend	good but not good enough – funny but not funny
Agent	beautiful – the oil and the machine – let's talk audiences – the first thing that has to be said about an audience is – fuck every last one of them – who the fuck do they think they are walking into my place and demanding to be made laugh – you want to laugh you

should've married someone who makes you
laugh you fucker – or better still go through
life with a happy disposition – audiences –
can't do without them can't shoot them –
now – where does that leave us – what we
do has nothing to do with them – the
responsibility is ours – we gauge audiences
so they can gauge us – what's good for a
comedy store in a back street at midnight –
but – never forget the material is yours –
without any judgement on anything let's
take an example from your appropriate set
tonight – do we need to tell long gags about
complete cunts – my immediate answer to
that is yes of course we do – i would have
to say in my mind he wasn't enough of a
complete cunt – and also i think it threw the
logic of the joke off – but anyway – for here
good – now – the question becomes if we
move on to a bigger audience is there any
way of telling the same gag without running
the risk of – and i hate this word – offending
some of the audience to the extent that they
don't find it funny – it's a question – a fucking
good question – it's not one that you have
to answer now but you need to think about
it – to my mind your best stuff is when you
briefly mentioned relationships – where's
this where's that – great stuff – beautiful –
common touch – just my opinion – normally
an agent would at a meeting like this lay
out his or her plan – the proposed tour or
whatever – i don't do that – if the truth be
told those things don't actually really matter –
any fuckwit can organise a tour – i need you
steve – i need both of you – to know – and

i mean to really know – that i know what
i'm talking about – that i know comedy –
i know this fucking business – you need to
trust me – and i need you to base that trust
on what i've just said – i know these are
important decisions – you have to talk
about it – of course you do – i'll wait
outside – give you a few minutes – don't
rush – if it's meant to be it's meant to be

The Agent exits but is still there.

Girlfriend   what the fuck was that

Comedian   i don't know what the fuck it was but he's
class

Girlfriend   we have to talk about this

Comedian   why

Girlfriend   i don't know we just do – who the fuck
smells people

Comedian   we all do

Girlfriend   i don't like him

Comedian   you don't have to like him – i do

Girlfriend   i know that – that's not what i meant – he
feels – he feels dangerous actually – that's
what i think

Comedian   look he's talking about the possibility of big
changes – talk like that always feels –
y'know – not dangerous – but y'know – scary

Girlfriend   you're not listening – not change is scary –
i know that – i'm an adult – i've changed
along the way – it was scary – he – that
man – feels dangerous

Comedian	i don't know what you're saying
Girlfriend	i don't know – i just sense something
Comedian	two things – fuck what you sense and . . .
Girlfriend	easy tiger – don't be getting ahead of yourself here – we're still at the stage where this is about the both of us
Comedian	i won't let it ever move on to a stage when it isn't about us – that was point two
Girlfriend	there's an atmosphere around him – you can nearly see it
Comedian	maybe that's what risk looks like
Girlfriend	maybe – or maybe it's what conflict looks like
Comedian	risk – there was always going to be a risk – well – it's arrived – that's what you sense
Girlfriend	there might be others – he's just the first – if he's that keen he'd wait
Comedian	does he look like a man who waits
Girlfriend	a good agent would tell you to shop around
Comedian	it's to do with what he said about my work – he knew what i was talking about – he had a feel for it – he was talking about moulding the material – that's it – i can talk with this man – that's it – really
Girlfriend	ok – (*Calls.*) mister wright
	The Agent enters.
Agent	backstage in these places – it's depressing – not conducive to good work i think – by the way i should've said earlier – i don't know –

i might be the first agent you've seen – you
should shop around – see what's out there –
it needs to be a good fit – you don't have
to want to sleep with me but you need to
know you can come to me and talk about
your work and i'll understand what you're
talking about – so if you want to get back to
me don't think i'll be – fucked off – i won't

Girlfriend   that sounds like a good . . .

Comedian   no it's fine mister wright . . .

Agent   doug – mister wright was my father

Comedian   was he an agent – are you following in his
footsteps

Agent   he was a butcher – spent his life surrounded
by dead meat – the opposite of what i do –
he killed things – i breathe life into them –
so – steve – what's it to be

Comedian   yes

Agent   excellent

Comedian   what's the next stage now – do you – i don't
know – what

Agent   maybe tomorrow come round to my office –
we'll talk

Comedian   is there a contract – do i sign something

Agent   no – nothing to sign – if you want a contract
i can draft one – but i don't usually – a
gentleman's agreement – i take the normal
percentage – it's all very straightforward –
we'll talk – we should go out for a drink –
celebrate

Comedian	of course
Agent	i can't – other business – but i want you to – i'll pay for it
Comedian	no don't be ridiculous
Agent	i insist
	Gives the Comedian money.
	it's my pleasure to do it
Comedian	thank you – that's very generous of you
Girlfriend	yes very generous
Agent	it's an investment – i'm a businessman
Comedian	i like what you have here – your office – it says something
Agent	big doesn't suit everybody – it suits me – thank you for coming alone – i know that might've been an issue
Comedian	maggie understands – a lot of glitz
Agent	i like glitz – it's not important but i like it – maggie – maggie – do you love her
Comedian	yes – did you start from nothing
Agent	yes
Comedian	why comedy
Agent	laughter's infectious – single saleable units
Comedian	so it's money then – you – it's money
Agent	yes – and laughter – i need to talk to you about maggie
Comedian	i said she's fine – or eventually she'll be fine – not totally sure what her journey is in all

	this y'know – worried about just becoming part of my story and not having one of her own
Agent	this relationship is between me and you – it's like a marriage – some people can be married to more than one person at a time – mormons i think you call them – some can't
Comedian	are you asking me to get rid of her
Agent	no – of course not – i would never ask or even suggest such a thing – i'm only your agent – there's more to life than work – i'm only bringing this to your attention so you arc aware of it – you need to think about these things – i don't know – maybe maggie has been guiding you – and given the circumstances why wouldn't she – all i'm saying is – you know what i'm saying – you're not stupid
Comedian	maggie and i are together
Agent	i know that
Comedian	is your father still alive
Agent	no
Comedian	your mother
Agent	no – ok i can see where this is going – i get it – i like it – i see your thinking – good plan
Comedian	no plan – no fucking plan – i just wanted to know something about you other than what's in front of me
Agent	you're good – you're very good
Comedian	don't play me

Agent	as you already know both my parents are dead – they were normal hard working people – i grew up in a normal hard working house – i have a brother and sister both of whom i've lost touch with – not through desire or design – we just – i don't know – drifted – stupid way of putting that – but – last i heard i think they were leading normal hard working lives – my brother's a teacher and my sister's – i've forgotten – maybe works in prisons talking to people – i don't know – i don't think a lot about that aspect of my life so i don't have much to say about it – i'm trying to think of something that explains myself to you – i'm always moving forward – i leave the past for others to deal with – how that affects you is that there is no point in either blaming or praising me – i'm always moving on – forward – i understand there are times when you need to do both those things – and by all means feel free – i shall of course take no notice – because you are in a relationship i'm assuming you might want to know if i am – no – i have never been married and have no children – and i have no time for people who follow that with – not that i know of – that's it
Comedian	do you want to know about me
Agent	i already know all i need to know about you – it's all there in your act – what i need to know is what it is you want – simply put
Comedian	success
Agent	one man's success is another man's failure – what type

Comedian	the type you provide
Agent	good answer
Comedian	but on my own terms
Agent	of course – there is no other way of doing this – everything must always be on your own terms – it's how i work – the best way to explain this is in terms of square footage – what were the measurements of the stage you were on the other night – i'd say twelve by ten – one hundred and twenty square feet – that's too small for you – too small for your thoughts – too small for your jokes – too small for your talent – we need to find you the right square footage – you need to be free to move – your act needs room to breathe – your thoughts – your words – they need space – they need time to land on people – your thoughts and words about them and how they live landing on them – we're talking big square footage there – have to work our way up to it of course – with each step forward each stage bigger – i love this feeling – the beginning of the journey – there's a sense of greatness in the air – can you smell that
Comedian	good evening ladies and gentlemen – my name's steve and i'll be your flight attendant for the evening – being on a plane is all about making sure you don't think about the notion that if this plane crashes i'm fucked – i love the idea that a whistle is going to save me – the whistle isn't for every possible disaster – it's only for use if crashing into water or some type of sporting event –

someone told me sharks don't sleep – just
continuously roaming the seas looking for
food – evolution – using whatever they can
to get their dinner – i'd imagined since the
first plane took to the skies to know that
their ears have become attuned to the sound
of whistles – dinner dinner dinner – fucking
whistles – all that economy airlines stuff
now you've to bring your own whistle – like
bringing your own knife and fork with you
if you were going to dine with the silence of
the lambs guy – they can't tell you the truth –
if they told you the truth fewer people
would fly – same as politicians – if they told
you the truth fewer people would vote for
the fuckers – there's a noise politicians make
when they're stuck – (*Makes noise.*) ever
hear it – why did the country go to war
against the wishes of the people – (*Noise.*)
is it true that you seek advice from god –
(*Noise.*) why do you continuously say
your political life is devoted to helping the
poor when what you actually do at every
possible opportunity is blame them for their
unfortunate situation while at the same time
praising the perpetual greed of the rich –
(*Noise.*) is it true that recently you said the
poorer in our society should tighten their
belts while you live as you please – (*Noise.*)
jesus christ – the government and the media
in any society that was worth living in or
fighting for should stand up to the powerful
and the wealthy – instead what do they do
here – they target the poor and the voiceless –
it's mainly the government but they get
certain sections of the media to spread the

word – i read these figures the other day –
not exact but near enough – polls suggest –
i know i don't need to explain this but i'm
going to anyway – polls as in surveys not
punters from poland – although maybe the
two are of like mind – who knows – and it's
quite possible that there's views from the
poles in the polls – polls suggest – that
people on average think that twenty seven
per cent of social security is lost to fraud –
when it is just point seven per cent – and that
forty one per cent goes to the unemployed
when it is actually only three per cent – why
do people think that – because aspects of
the media do the government's dirty work
for them – politicians have become the
scourge of the earth – they have made every
aspect of our lives political – education
health religion sport culture – every fucking
thing – and in doing that they've ruined every
fucking one of them – not content with that
they send the young to meaningless fucking
wars to die in some foreign field for an
invented cause they know nothing about –
no dignity in those deaths – just sorry –
can't give you a straight answer – imagine
we were to do that in our normal or working
lives – did you press the switch i told you
not to press and in doing so caused one eyed
john to lose his hand in the cutting stuff
with a very sharp blade machine – (*Noise.*)
did you drink all the vodka knowing fine
well that i like a glass first thing in the
morning you greedy bastard – (*Noise.*) did
you leave those slippers in the middle of the
hall – did you leave the cat out all night –

did you the leave the fucking remote in the room with no fucking tv in it – (*Noise.*) that noise would cause bloodshed – total carnage – relationships seem to be based on how we handle where the people we love leave stuff – did you leave that empty juice carton back in the fridge – it would be an easier question to answer and cause less friction if you were asked at that moment – did you fuck the next door neighbour – yes i did actually – i'm sorry – i should've told you – it was just a one off thing – it meant nothing – i still and will always love you – it was a mistake – all i can say is sorry – it's ok i know you love me and we all make mistakes – thank you for being so understanding – it's ok i know you would do the same for me – did you put that empty juice carton back in the fridge – yes – sorry – sorry – fucking sorry – what demented type of a fuck puts an empty carton back in the fucking fridge – it was a mistake – mistake – a fucking mistake – it's not a mistake it's a state of mind – a mistake is fucking marrying you – what this is has to do with the very core of your being – an incident – incident – that's not even the right word – it doesn't have within it the fucking magnitude of what is wrong with what you did – i can't even bring myself to repeat it you dirty fucker – this tells me that you can't be trusted and you don't care – i can't talk about it – i need space – i just can't – fuck – small things – we can handle the big things – i'm pregnant – i know we weren't planning for it and it isn't a good time but –

we can't handle the small things – did i just
see you wiping your dick on the fucking
good curtains – the good curtains – that's a
strange concept – we can eventually if we
try hard afford good curtains – you keep the
good curtains for the good room don't you –
there'd be no point in having the good
curtains in the room we live in that looks
like a shit heap – there has to be continuity –
good room good curtains – shit heap room
shit heap curtains – or if it's a real shit heap
no fucking curtains at all – actually if you
were thinking straight you'd put the good
curtains over that window so no one could
see in and see what type of person you
really are – the good room – when i was
young the people that were brought into the
good room were cunts – priests and well to
do relatives – the type of fuckers that make
you question yourself in a bad way – yet at
the same time never ask themselves anything
of worth – the type of person that made
you want to have a good room in the first
place – even though you couldn't afford it
was a waste of a good room and made you
embarrassed about the rest of the house –
on a very basic level we're meant to elect
leaders who are meant to stop that from
happening – but they don't – it suits them
that we don't trust ourselves – that we don't
have any confidence in our own judgement
about every fucking decision we make about
every fucking thing in the whole fucking
world – you see where we are right now –
and given what's happening to us day and
daily i don't understand why there isn't a

revolution – well i do actually – we're afraid
to lose the little amount of shit that we
own – we're afraid that some fucker with no
shit will take our shit while we're out on the
streets protesting against the man and trying
to make the entire fucking planet a better
place for all future generations – protesters
are nuts now aren't they – it's all tree bark
whale sperm and the rights of unborn snow
tigers to vote in the north pole general
elections – where the big issue is – snow –
good or bad thing – are snow tigers in the
north pole – i made that up – i've no idea –
starting to make stuff up – what's that
about – you see anyone who tells you that
snow tigers are important and at the same
time cuts funds from the local maternity
hospital tell them to fuck off and live with
the snow tigers – i see some of you are going
with the snow tiger thing and others are
thinking – don't know – lovely wee white
furry baby snow tigers – comedy's a risky
business – i'm going to finish off with a joke –
for no other reason only than i like it – and
to remind you that i am a comic – so you
better fucking laugh at this – especially you
in the front row – a man wants to buy a
racehorse – he doesn't know how to go
about that so the first thing he does is look
in the bought and sold section of his local
newspaper – as chance would have it there
is indeed a racehorse for sale in the local
newspaper – a city centre paper – you know
the type – the south whatever post – someone
pulled the flowers up in the park a picture of
a couple who've been married for a hundred

years and the under elevens win the cup for
the first time in eleven years – racehorse for
sale enquiries to fifty five walmer street –
this man lives in the next street to walmer
street – kimberly street – all terraced houses
and yards so he thinks this can't be right but
i'll call round anyway – calls to the house
and an old woman he has never seen before –
and he thought he knew everyone in the
area because he was a nosey bastard –
answers – racehorse – yes yes yes – do you
keep it in the country – no i keep it out in
the yard – i want to buy a racehorse – i
know that – i want to sell a racehorse – the
man thinks this old woman is not the full
shilling but decides to have a look anyway –
there is indeed a racehorse in the yard – it
has a beat up head a dopey look and a
curved spine – this isn't a racehorse – yes it
is – was – is – was – is – the old woman
opens the yard door and outside is a huge
field – the man even though he has lived in
this area all his life has never seen this field
before – in the far corner of the field there is
a single oak tree – the old woman slaps the
horse on the arse and the horse bolts out of
the yard and into the field at the speed of
light – this is the fastest horse god ever
pumped breath into – the man is thinking
i'm going to make a fortune here – the old
woman isn't going to know what it's worth
and i'll get odds on that hairy old bastard
winning anything – he was thinking of how
he was going to spent the money – a holiday
for the family – a new car – maybe get
himself a mistress – one of those mail order

ones – set her up in a flat – go round at the
weekends – split a chinese with her and
have a ride – just as he was thinking that the
horse ran straight smack into the oak tree
and collapses in a heap – that's the fastest
horse i've ever seen in my life he says but
tell me why does it run into the oak tree –
i don't know the old woman says – he just
doesn't give a fuck – thank you – you've
been a delightful audience – good night and
good luck

Agent   yes yes – good stuff – minor suggestion –
lose the stats – factual – true – all that stuff –
audiences don't want to think they're going
to a lecture – only a minor suggestion

Girlfriend   i think he should keep them in plus i don't
like the way he tells that joke any more –
i'm not sure i liked it to begin with – but the
way he tells it now isn't him – there's no
point in this if he's not being himself – if
he's not himself where's the thought coming
from – nowhere – he'll get caught

Agent   the audience seemed to like it

Girlfriend   the audience – comedy isn't just about the
audience – well it is and it isn't – you're
taking something from him

Agent   i'm giving him something – i'm giving him
what he wanted – an opportunity – whether
he takes that or not is up to himself – the
question is – should you be getting in the
way of that

Girlfriend   i know him

Agent	i don't doubt that for a second – you have to allow for change – what is the point in any of this if we don't allow someone we love to change – we all struggle with that – i understand – we see something we like so we want it to stay the same – he is evolving – you either stay in the background and watch that happen – or – you leave
Girlfriend	i might want to stay and guide
Agent	that might help at the start – when things start to heat up that's a hindrance – we both want the same thing don't we
Girlfriend	i don't think so – in fact i know we don't
Agent	for a second stop thinking i'm the enemy
Girlfriend	that's how the enemy wins though isn't it – when you stop thinking they're the enemy and they do what they want anyway
Agent	ok – it's only fuckin comedy you know
Girlfriend	it's all he has – and me
Agent	ok – i'm the enemy – you make peace with your enemies don't you – we'll follow that line of thinking
Girlfriend	you don't know what he's been through to get here
Agent	i don't need to know – and between you and me nor do i care – it's a tough business – blah blah – weep weep weep – do you follow boxing
Girlfriend	what do you think

Agent	i think that you just became predictable which says a lot – maybe your predictability is holding him back – just hold that thought while i tell you about the boxing – i'm not a boxing fan but i can understand why it exists – like most things if you ask people about boxers they'd be able to name a few – all very famous – because they only know the best ones it gives them a false impression of what boxing is – they don't see or are aware of the reality of it – for every successful boxer there is – and there are few – there are hundreds who fight week in and week out for next to nothing – week in week out they get the shit beat out of them – all of them waiting – waiting for that opportunity – waiting for someone like me to wipe the blood and sweat from their face and take them by the hand to what might possibly be a shot at the title – you can't tell me that's not what they want – because what the fuck would they be doing it for if they didn't – why would they put themselves through that if it wasn't for the possibility of a shot – the point is normal punters don't really need to know that – but we do – so stop fucking whining about nothing and start seeing the real picture – you know we don't want the same thing – stop thinking that – the point is we should
Girlfriend	your problem is you think because i don't like you i don't understand you
Agent	i don't have a problem and i don't give a fuck what you think

Girlfriend	my turn – to carry on with your ridiculous boxing analogy
Agent	i think you're weakening – ridiculous is a soft word
Girlfriend	no i'm not
Agent	yes you are
Girlfriend	go fuck yourself
Agent	come on you're better than that
Girlfriend	whenever you wipe the blood and sweat from the boxer's face and you say do you want a shot at the title – you don't at the same time say – but you have to change your style – the style that got you noticed – the style that got you this far
Agent	i think you do
Girlfriend	i won't let you
Agent	it's not up to you
Girlfriend	we'll see
Comedian	not sure about the joke at the end
Agent	i think it works
Girlfriend	i don't
Agent	more people get it
Girlfriend	it's lost its edge
Comedian	i want more people to get it without it losing its edge
Agent	i have a suggestion – we need to move forward – we're looking for the new thing but at the same time it feels comfortable –

of course this is entirely up to yourself – it's only a suggestion – i'm only here to guide – it's you that makes the real decisions

Girlfriend we can listen to this some other time – let's go for a drink – it's been a long day

Comedian no i want to here it

Agent just think about it – all you have to do is think about it – run a marathon for charity.

Girlfriend the marathon – the fucking marathon – do you not see what's happening here – breakfast presenters – sad bad glad – what's the line – remember the line – they don't really want to tell you anything other than they have just ran the marathon – just numbing the fuck out of everything – it's not just how or what steve it's why it's about fucking why – our journey is about why – i'm here because of why – run the fucking marathon for charity.

Agent it doesn't actually have to be a marathon and it doesn't actually have to be for charity – really what you're talking about is some feat of endurance to highlight the injustice in the world – children are good – or poor people in countries where you're never going to do a gig – the beauty about that is it's not important whether they think you're funny or not – it's the same with the children – they're poor and they need stuff – funny isn't important – it's not about that anyway – it gets your name known – not for being a comedian but for being a good person – and that's the kicker – now i'm not suggesting for a second that you have to become a

good person – all i'm talking about is the
notion that people think you are – this all
has to do with trust – let's assume you're on
the verge of doing big gigs – which we know
you will be – people are out working all week
doing whatever shitty job it is they do – they
pay hard earned cash to go and watch a
funny man – they're ready – waiting – they
want you to deliver the goods – my point is
they'll be more inclined to listen to you if
they think you're a good person

Girlfriend   don't even think about this – not for a
second should you let that thought creep
into your mind

Comedian   it has to be thought about – everything has
to be thought about

Girlfriend   i'm not listening to this

She begins to exit.

Comedian   please don't go – i don't see what's wrong
with wanting to be a good person anyway

Agent   exactly – is there anything like that you feel
you could endure

Comedian   i used to play table tennis

Agent   no – we need you to look strong and caring –
not look like a – what's the word – dickhead –
you don't have to be any good at it – what
the fuck is running anyway – it's just
walking quickly – swimming – man against
the elements – bikes – you see the good
thing about the marathon is it's man against
himself – that's what makes people think
you're honest – and in comedy as you well

49

know that's gold dust – i'm thinking maybe –
i'm wondering – maybe you could lie – all
the good ones do this – they make up shit
that sounds as if it actually happened – you
know cute stories about their kids and the
funny names they have – i don't know –
stories about them being on planes and
something funny happened on the plane –
or jobs they pretended they had – that type
of shit – all i'm saying is think about it –
it'll help – i know it will

The middle of a gig.

Comedian running the marathon has changed my view
of nature – running for charity – not that
that matters – not a charity for nature –
people first nature second – it changed my
notion about the speed of animals – i was
running at what i thought was an average
human speed and i was passed by a duck a
horse and an elephant – the horse you would
expect – the elephant was a surprise – but a
duck – their feet aren't even made for
running for god's sake – couldn't catch him
either – although in saying that there were
ducks everywhere so it mightn't have been
the same one – not sure that i've been that
close to a duck before but when you see
them on tv they don't seem to be moving
that quickly – nor do they look that big –
it was a human won the race by the way –
must've been moving some to beat a horse –
maybe the horse fell – i don't know –
personally i don't get animals – but i like the
whole notion that we run together – not
sure what would happen if an animal won it

though – the winner gets money – i mean –
what would that be about – couldn't spend
it – would have nowhere to put it – the
animals haven't thought that through have
they – maybe they're not in it for the money –
maybe animals know something we don't –
some of you are going – yes yes that's right –
animals are closer to god than us they are
on a higher spiritual plan – they understand
our place in the world – that could be true
but then we have the guns – and drugs –
who wouldn't want those things – if you
could have them why wouldn't you want
them – plus animals can't skip – very close
to talking about skipping now – give a man
enough rope – i've started going to the gym –
i drive to the gym get on a treadmill and
walk for the amount of time it would take
me to walk to the gym then i get in my car
and drive home – there's nothing strange
about that though because everyone in the
gym does that – i go during the day because
i work at night – you know that – you're
here – during the day is normally older
people – what's that about – older people –
the changing room is just skin and noises –
old naked men look as if they already have
clothes on them – there's something going
on with old men that defies some scientific
rule or something – they let out more air
than they take in – every movement air
escapes from somewhere – it escapes
sometimes from places that don't even have
any holes – although most of it escapes from
the holes – there was an old man sitting
beside me – i say sitting beside me i mean

drying what might have been his arse –
difficult to tell – with his t-shirt – over and
above the normal noises i could've sworn
i heard air coming out of his ears – ears –
arse – same letters – maybe as you get older
they actually connect themselves – my
girlfriend doesn't like me going to the gym –
she thinks movement like that is unnatural –
she thinks there are better ways to spend
your time – like not going to the gym –
women – i know i have to be careful here –
but – what's this no logic business – i can't
describe to you an argument between the
two of us because it's too complex to
put into words – it's like it takes place
within a universe where two contradictory
things exist within the one unit and they're
both right – a universe where nothing is
constant – nothing is straightforward –
everything is complex – even the things
that are straightforward – if they existed –
where all questions are answered with other
questions – a universe which is all questions
and no answers – it's like being involved in
some type of pure philosophical scientific
debate about the working life of a tea
towel – and then there's a record – a mental
journal – a journal that doesn't exist within
time – forever in the present – nothing is
forgotten – nothing – ever – don't think
i've forgotten that look you gave me on july
the third two thousand and two when i
asked you to put the bin out and you had
already done it – and yesterday – that tea
towel – it was nowhere near ready for the
wash basket – you did that on purpose –

	whenever you're wrong you do it on purpose whenever you're right it's by accident – i've been steve johnston – thank you and good night
Agent	i've got you a televised gig – short tour then bang – the big time – good set tonight – be careful about animals – people can be funny about god's creatures – really good stuff about maggie – spot on – thinking about the panel of a quiz show – not sure what one though – has to fit your personality and the type of funny man you are – and you are a funny man
Girlfriend	i'm not going with you on tour this time
Comedian	what
Girlfriend	i'm not going with you
Comedian	is this about doug
Girlfriend	no
Comedian	it is isn't it
Girlfriend	no
Comedian	you don't have to like him
Girlfriend	I know that
Comedian	you always go with me
Girlfriend	not this time
Comedian	this will be the best time yet – better hotels – more money – treat it like a holiday – do what you want during the day then go to the shows at night
Girlfriend	i don't want to go to the shows

Comedian	don't do this now
Girlfriend	you don't need me there
Comedian	yes i do – this is what we wanted
Girlfriend	you don't listen – it's what you wanted
Comedian	i don't want to discuss this
Girlfriend	you're right – neither do i
Comedian	no fuck it – say it
Girlfriend	i don't mind you going to the gym
Comedian	what
Girlfriend	i don't want to watch you do stand up any more – i don't like what you do
Comedian	are you going to leave me
Girlfriend	no
Comedian	you just can't watch me do my job
Girlfriend	yes
Comedian	i'm on my own
Girlfriend	where that's concerned yes
Comedian	this is the first step towards something isn't it
Girlfriend	i don't know – i haven't lived outside your comedy before – i don't know
Comedian	come with me
Girlfriend	this is your journey not mine – go on it – and maybe i'll be here when you return
Comedian	fuck you
Girlfriend	really – you want to be like that

Comedian	no
Girlfriend	you're a funny man
Agent	sorry to hear maggie won't be with you – but maybe it's for the best – need to knuckle down – focus on being funny – must be great to be funny

On tour.

Comedian	i don't know the old woman said – he just doesn't give a fuck – i've been steve johnston – thank you and good night
	i don't know the old woman says – he just doesn't give a fuck – i've been steve johnston thank you and good night.
	he just doesn't give a damn – i've been steve johnston thank you and good night
	he just doesn't give a damn – i've been steve johnston thank you and good night
	that sounds very cruel does it not – what do i care they're only bees – i've been steve johnston
	what do i care they're only bees – i've been steve johnston
	what do i care they're only bees – i've been steve johnston
	i've been steve johnston
Comedian	we need to talk
Agent	you're kidding me – we need to talk – what the fuck is this
Comedian	there's questions i need to ask you

Agent   ok – ok – look – i was expecting this – we're
at a crossroads – there's questions – important
questions – i'm the man that gave you what
you wanted because you told me that's what
you wanted – and now that it looks like it
might happen you think there's something
wrong – that you can't handle it – it's
understandable – i would suggest you're
looking for morality where none exists – i'm
going to come clean here – i will explain
who i am and what i do – after that it's your
choice – let's start with something simple
and we'll build our way up will we – this is
just a general point about morality – help
you understand me more maybe – as things
go on – if that is your choice – and the
crowds get bigger you'd imagine that every
so often there might be a woman in the
audience who if asked in the right way might
be prepared to go back stage after the gig
and give you a blowjob – before you get on
your high horse there i'm not suggesting
that's why you became a comedian – you're
a man of principles i get it – i'm just throwing
it out there as a possibility – so – a woman
you don't know is going to give you a
blowjob because you make her laugh and
to her are famous – two things about that –
there are some people who have a problem
with that but that's only because they don't
have the ability to allow themselves to get
blowjobs from strangers – they can't liberate
themselves – they use (*air quotes*) morality
in an attempt to keep the liberated down –
they suck the life out of the living so to
speak – my second point is the one i like

56

best – it has to do with free will – i'm a big
free willer – these same people will say that
woman is being used – and even if she doesn't
know it herself she is still being used – i can
think of nothing more condescending –
what they say is immediately after giving
you the blowjob she will hate herself for
having done it – an hour or so later she'll be
knocking back tequilas to get rid of the
imagined taste of your dick – or twenty
years later she wishes she wasn't the type of
woman who in her younger days gave funny
men blowjobs – here's the truth – because
i've talked to these women – i'm the one
who asks them to go backstage – asks them
by the way – nothing more than that – if
they say no they say no – i don't care – free
will – the truth is they don't give a fuck –
the blowjob and you are just part of a story
to be told – they know that and they're
happy enough with it – i like women like
that – women who know their own minds –
robust women – the point i'm making is a
simple one – you should be happy with a
job where you get blowjobs from women
who like what you do – the next point is a
more serious one and it's something you do
need to think about – have your comedians
clean and your politicians dirty – say there
was a bigger picture to all this – i'm not
saying there is but say there was – and
say i had a view on that – and say i am to
the devil what christians are to god –
neither one of those entities may exist by
the way – but that doesn't matter – people
misunderstand that situation i think – think

about it on a personal level – why would
anyone be interested in your poxy shitty
little soul – whatever happens happens here
on earth – don't panic about this by the way
– it's just a view – i'm drawn to the idea that
the world exists in a state of conflict –
division – suspicion – mistrust – governments
provide those things – and i think they
should be left alone to do that – like good
citizens then i think we should help with the
war effort or whatever the fuck it is at the
time – it isn't just war by the way it has to
do with rampant capitalism – you know
what i mean you get the picture – to help
that grow and thrive people need their
minds taken off it – that's where you and
the likes of you come in – i think it helps
that situation if two thousand people laugh
at the idea that we should all skip to work
or that women's behaviour confuses the
average man – the average man or woman
likes hearing about the average man or
woman – that's all that's happening here –
now – you don't have to buy into any of
that – that's just how i think – the point
is this – you have a decision to make – i think
what makes you tick is making people
laugh – and the more people you make
laugh – well you work it out – it's your
choice – here it's tv put that on

Hands him a remembrance poppy.

your audience awaits

Comedian   on my own – always on my own – i'm
funny – funny – funny – funny – the
big one – the more people the better –

58

straight in – audience – see what happens –
health – marathon – air flight – nature –
relationships – done before – in the bag –
you can do this – can do this – this is what
it's about – good clean polished set –
professional – professional – do it – fuck –
fuck – right – go

Pins the poppy to his jacket.

hello – is everyone happy – can't hear you –
is everyone happy – i'll soon put a stop to
that – a big crowd – big is better – all the
women in the audience who think big is
better put their hands up – not as many
as you think – i imagine that would be
different if there were no men here – all the
men looking and saying do not dare put
your hand up – i don't think that's true
anyway – bigger is better – not that i would
know entirely – better at this moment –
improve my lifestyle – i think what is meant
when women say bigger is better is the flip
side of that – all the men are thinking now
please god don't have another vote – it's not
bigger is better – it's – yes of course – small is
useless – so – all the women in the audience
who think small is useless put your hands
up – for the ten or so who put their hands
up i imagine you're here on your own – or
you're in town for a sex toys convention –
it's good to be here – the taxi driver who
brought me here once i told him what i was
doing told me a joke and said i should use
it – i don't normally tell jokes – which is a
bit risky for a comedian i understand – but
i thought i'd give this one a go – taxi drivers

can be intimidating can't they – they have
the knowledge you don't – that's not the
joke by the way – the annual honey festival
is taking place in some place somewhere –
and the three beekeepers with the best honey
are getting their awards – different coloured
jars i think – they're all interviewed
afterwards – people who are curious about
these things want to know about the number
of hives and the amount of bees and that –
the third guy is asked – he has ten thousand
bees and he keeps them in one hundred
hives – the second guy is asked and he has
fifty thousand bees and he keeps them in
five hundred hives – they ask the guy who has
won the cup for best honey – why is your
honey so good – it must have something to
do with your bee hive ratio – so tell us –
how many bees you have and how many
hives you have – he says one million bees
and one hive – one million bees and just one
hive – that sounds very cruel does it not –
what do i care they're only bees – so that's
the type of things taxi drivers think about –
a few beekeepers in by the sound of it – by
the way just in case some of you don't know
this is being filmed tonight – tv – we're all
going to be on tv – i can hear the groans
now – some of the women are disgusted
because the cameras are here and they didn't
put their best gear on – what can i say – it's
not always about you sometimes it's about
me – so all be on your best behaviour –
that includes you – don't panic – it's always
your worst nightmare when you buy tickets
in the front row – or your boyfriend buys

them – not looking good for you tonight
son – i notice you didn't put your hand up
for either vote there – so everything ok in
that department – as far as you can tell –
fair enough – that leaves the situation in the
balance i think – and on top of that tickets
in the front row – where the bad man can
accost you about the satisfaction you may
or may not feel regarding the size of your
boyfriend's penis – no need to panic – i just
needed a link – so – i take it this is your
boyfriend – how long have you been going
out – three years – so getting near that point
where you have to make a decision – i'm
not saying you have to make it now – so
relationships –

He moves back to middle of stage.

see what i just did there – there's a craft to
this you know – it's never about the big
things it's always about the small things –
small things like breathing – i'm at that
stage now where i look at her and think if
i'd a' murdered you i'd be out by now and
a free man – don't get me wrong she thinks
like that too – our relationship is based on
equality – where did you leave the car keys –
who would've thought that tiny question
means so much – where did you leave the
car keys means – you have ruined my life –
every moment i am with you you drain the
life from me – if only i had the courage i'd
hold a pillow over your face until your feet
stopped kicking – and as i say that works
both ways – because the answer to the
question – where did you leave the car keys –

is – in the car key bowl where i always leave
them – the two in the front row aren't doing
much laughing now – and what i've been
talking about is the good part – long term
relationships or partnerships – that always
feels a bit too businesslike for me – a lot of
meetings and votes taken – or marriage – or
whatever it is you kids are calling it today
are based on a couple's ability to outlive
each other through spite – that is the natural
way of things – a law of nature – to want to
outlive the person you love – dash – hate so
you can dance on – stroke – weep over their
grave keeps you going – it takes the place of
exercise – although in saying that i've started
to use both spite and exercise – i don't
know whether you know or not but i run
the odd marathon now and again – ah – you
have heard – what have a horse an elephant
and a duck all got in common – they are
all better marathon runners than i am –
it's very disconcerting being passed by a
duck – the horse you expect – the elephant
is a surprise – but the duck – it upsets the
whole balance of nature – because you
believe in the possibility of it – and you
can't understand it – it flies in the face of
everything you've been told about ducks –
you see if it was a snail there would be no
problem because you would realise you
were in a dream or a child's book and think
nothing more of it – but a duck – hands up
here anyone who runs marathons – some –
keep your hands up if you are continuously
beaten by ducks – and i don't mean physically
attacked by ducks – there was a guy there

who had his hand up for that and then took
it down – have you done something to upset
the duck community – i didn't know there
was a duck community – if there is that's
truly frightening – that might account for
them making a concerted effort to win the
marathon – so some of you know what i
mean – you've been passed by a duck – it's
crazy – elephants are the only other animals
to get drunk – did you know that – although
i just want to state for the record that none
of the elephants that run past me are drunk –
they couldn't be – they have to do a drug
test just like the rest of us – they always
have a very bemused look on their faces
when they have to take the test – i don't
know why – probably thinking it would be
more fun to run this drunk – so why don't
the humans – i'm sure that's not what they
call us – should just let us do that – drunk
elephants and super fast ducks – it would be
chaos – in connection with that i've started
to go to the gym – being full of spite of
course my girlfriend can't understand that –
i go during the day – during the day is
mainly old people – which is good for me
for within that world i'm a duck – i'm a
duck – a duck – old people's bodies are
funny aren't they – no offence to any older
people here – but what's going on there –
it's going to happen to us all – so – for some
reason old people don't care if you see them
naked – either they have bigger issues to
deal with like death or like vampires they
don't do mirrors – either way they prance
around the changing rooms with gay

abandon – and that includes the ones that
are actually gay – they have extra skin –
they have extra skin – right – sorry – also
more air comes out of them than goes into
them – and they make noises every time
they move – so basically old age is all skin
air and noise – funny thing about the gym –
ah – i drive there and then walk on a
treadmill for the same amount of time it
would've taken me to walk to the gym – no
i don't – i don't do that – bring the house
lights up – bring the house lights up

The house lights are brought up.

i don't own a car – i don't own a car – i don't
own a car – i don't own a car – i can drive –
i have driven but i don't now – i passed
my test first pop when i was about twenty
three – drove for about six months then
stopped – nothing happened – i didn't crash
or lose my licence – i just stopped – i didn't
trust myself behind the wheel of a car –
driving is like swimming – you do it yourself
and you take responsibility for it – i don't
swim either – i can a bit but only a bit – the
point is i just told you i drive to the gym
and i don't – i did go to the gym – i don't go
any more but i remember what it was like –
my girlfriend used to drive me there – but
she's not with me any more so i don't bother
going – even though she's not with me any
more i remember what it's like to have a
girlfriend – to be in a relationship – to argue
about where the car keys are – or to imagine
what an argument about where the car keys
might be – i don't run marathons any more –

not that i ran that many – i remember what
it's like to run them though – wasn't ever
beaten by a duck – the reason i told you i
drive to the gym was because it allowed me
to say that the time i spend in the gym is
roughly the same time it would take me to
walk to and from the gym – the gag is about
not noticing what you're doing in life –
instead of spending all that time in the gym
and all that money why didn't i just walk
there and back – it would have the same
effect exercise wise – that's not right though –
i didn't think the logic of it through – i don't
just walk on a treadmill at the gym i do
other exercises more vigorous than walking –
so what i was getting at doesn't make any
sense – i told you a lie for a gag that doesn't
work – i understand it's not that funny to
begin with – even in among other material
it is only on the cusp of mildly funny –
running – i should've said running instead
of walking – instead of driving to the gym
i should've run to the gym – and back – still
on the cusp – but maybe then the lie was
worth it – this is all i have – here now –
i can't do anything else – this is it – bring
the lights down.

The house lights are brought down.

i was on a plane the other week – this is an
insight into how men think – i was bored
so i started reading the plastic safety sheet –
you know the drawing on it it's like a
cartoon really – of the air hostess putting on
the life jacket – whatever position she was
in – i thought to myself – i'd have sex with

her – two things about that – it's a two d
drawing that doesn't exist in the real world –
doesn't exist as an actual woman i mean –
and – with that knowledge in mind – if i was
on a plane tomorrow – which i might well
be because i'm going places – i'd have the
same thought again – that's what you're
dealing with girls – i like the whistles on the
life jackets – i think that's a great idea – it
does two things – and this is the genius of
it both of which you wouldn't necessarily
have thought of them yourself – evolution
being what it is i'm positive by now sharks
have worked out what the sound of that
whistle means – i like the next one even
more though – if the sharks know what that
noise means i imagine the other flyers who
are floating on top of the ocean in the dead
of night know what it means when that
noise stops – it means there is no doubt any
more there are definitely sharks – and they're
now heading for you – if the truth be told
people on planes instead of whistles they
should be given guns – although i suppose
that opens up a whole other can of worms –
if a worm passed you while running the
marathon it would be the same as a snail –
although instead of dreaming you might
think that you'd accidently taken crack
cocaine – which of course would make the
elephants jealous – runners always have a
pained look on their face – it's that same look
you see on men shopping in supermarkets –
every decision and action is a pain in the ass
– i don't know – it's milk – milk's milk –
what do you want me to say – does it have

to be grated or sliced can you just not get it
in a block – i don't know i just don't like
green grapes – i don't ask you questions like
that – i don't have to think about it i don't
like them – yes maybe it is because my
mother was too lenient on me when i was
young and didn't force feed me the green
grapes – why do we need them anyway they
just sit there – yes i know – i get it – it's so
people coming to the house think we are the
type of people who eat green grapes – no
one comes to the house – eggs are eggs and
they're only chickens – they're only bees –
he just doesn't give a – boom boom – my
girlfriend insists on going to that self service
checkout thing – before you even get to
the machine you can see that it's smiling –
the place empties of staff because they're
all watching a monitor somewhere – we've
got one – sandwiches – tea – monitor –
entertainment for the day – you have to
approach the machine with confidence or
you're dead in the water – three hours later –
crying – police – groceries everywhere – first
mistake – put the wrong bag down in the
packing area – the machine doesn't recognise
the bag – why would it they haven't met
before – didn't realise we had to bring bags
with us that the machine had previously
dated – what happens then is i follow its
pattern – it keeps saying don't recognise the
bag – i keep saying go to a real checkout –
don't recognise the bag – go to a real
checkout – don't recognise the bag – go to a
real checkout – the girlfriend then says to
me look what you've done now you've

upset it – doesn't take my side – doesn't
matter that it's upset me – i give the machine
a look – a look that says if i ever meet you
outside this place it's game over – bad
move – first up – loose apples – the machine
can't believe its luck – loose apples – i turn
to her – really – you can see the situation
here and you want to start off with loose
apples – it then dawns on me what's
happening here – the two of them are in
cahoots – why else are we here – and don't
think i don't know what's going on here –
it's punishment – i was told about this – my
father warned me – he said no matter what
you do in life within a relationship always
be careful where you put stuff – and – think
about the condition you've left the stuff in –
i've tried my best – but this one time i got
confused – for any man trying to remember
to do two things at once – you know –
you're as likely to make gold from base
metal – women of course – sometimes it
looks like they have more limbs than they
actually have the amount of stuff they're
doing – another thing too – this incident –
this wrongdoing – happened well over a
year ago – that in itself shows you the
severity of the crime – so i think i might've
been confused – not about location but
about condition – so it was in the right
place but the wrong condition – two things
about that – i thought location was
more important than condition – wrong –
two entirely different things that exist
independently of each other – which means
you can be one hundred per cent wrong

about both – or either – the other thing was
i don't think i fully understood the entire or
complete definition or total meaning of –
condition – in my head i thought it had to
do with an object's appearance – no – not
just outer but also inner – not just the body
but also the soul – when you think about it
that's a beautiful thought – that a person
sees another person in their entirety – we
can all see how that would make the world
a better place – i didn't realise – and in a
way this is my fault – i didn't realise that i
had to deal with inanimate objects – stuff –
at that level – it's an easy mistake – but still
one you need to be punished for a year or so
later – i put an empty carton of orange back
in the fridge – i know what you're thinking –
why – to be honest i can't remember why –
i know it wasn't out of spite or to torture
her because i'd remember that – i have since
thought long and hard about this and all
that i can come up with is that i maybe
couldn't have been bothered to put it in the
place i should've put it – the bin – which is
outside – to make matters worse whenever
i was quizzed about it i made this noise –
(*Makes the noise.*) that noise has to do with
not being able to answer – so you just go –
(*Noise.*) why is there an empty orange juice
carton in the fridge – (*Noise.*) so we're at
the self service and she puts the loose apples
on the machine – and i get this look – no
words just a look – but the look has words
and the words are – go on make that noise
now – thank you – i've been steve johnston

To black.